AF207718

COLOR YOUR YOUR CAREER

A Positive Affirmation
Coloring Book | Second Edition

CAREER HORIZONS

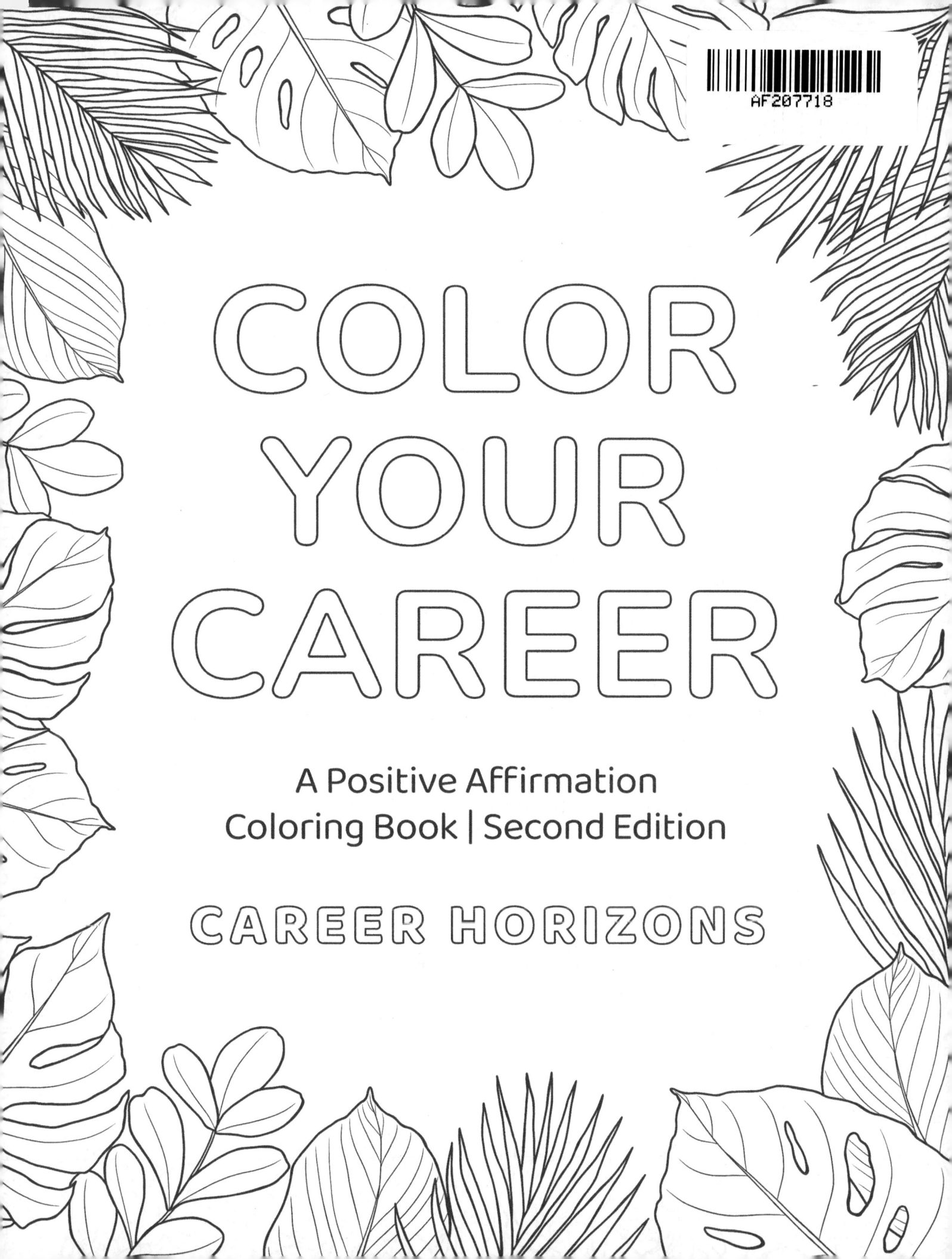

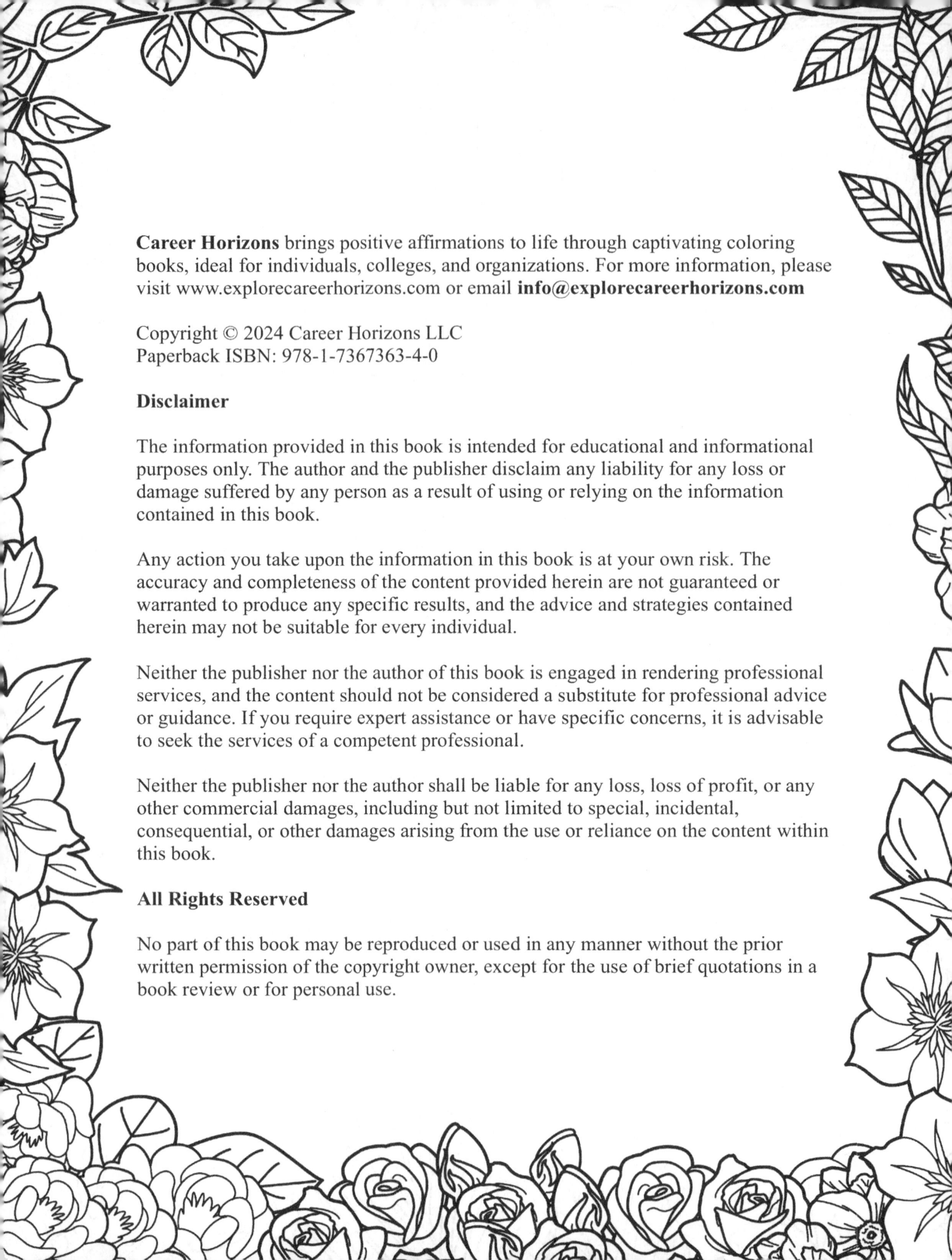

Career Horizons brings positive affirmations to life through captivating coloring books, ideal for individuals, colleges, and organizations. For more information, please visit www.explorecareerhorizons.com or email **info@explorecareerhorizons.com**

Copyright © 2024 Career Horizons LLC
Paperback ISBN: 978-1-7367363-4-0

Disclaimer

The information provided in this book is intended for educational and informational purposes only. The author and the publisher disclaim any liability for any loss or damage suffered by any person as a result of using or relying on the information contained in this book.

Any action you take upon the information in this book is at your own risk. The accuracy and completeness of the content provided herein are not guaranteed or warranted to produce any specific results, and the advice and strategies contained herein may not be suitable for every individual.

Neither the publisher nor the author of this book is engaged in rendering professional services, and the content should not be considered a substitute for professional advice or guidance. If you require expert assistance or have specific concerns, it is advisable to seek the services of a competent professional.

Neither the publisher nor the author shall be liable for any loss, loss of profit, or any other commercial damages, including but not limited to special, incidental, consequential, or other damages arising from the use or reliance on the content within this book.

All Rights Reserved

No part of this book may be reproduced or used in any manner without the prior written permission of the copyright owner, except for the use of brief quotations in a book review or for personal use.

This book belongs to:

OPPORTUNITIES

Doors open easily for me

JOB OFFERS FLOW TO ME WITH EASE

FUTURE

INTERVIEW

MONEY

My income
INCREASES
every year

MONEY follows me wherever I go

Made in the USA
Middletown, DE
04 February 2025

70328849R00031